CAREER AS A

FORENSIC ACCOUNTANT

IF YOU LEARN HOW TO FOLLOW THE money, it could lead you to a career in forensic accounting.

Though mystery and intrigue are not words usually associated with the field of accounting, the profession does have a more adventurous side, and it's known as forensic accounting. Like other forensic work, which is usually done to ferret out wrongdoing in connection with criminal or civil investigations, forensic accounting calls for practitioners to dig deeper into a case than investigators ordinarily do and to challenge themselves to find cleverly concealed evidence.

Accounting sleuths look at financial records with a critical eye, disregarding what the numbers look like on the surface and determining what they really mean when the entire fiscal picture is pieced together and put into proper prospective. Forensic accounting involves believing that, while numbers never lie, they can be manipulated, and everything is not always as it appears.

With profits at the core of many criminal activities, law enforcement is relying more heavily than ever on the talents of accountants to help build cases against lawbreakers. Financial evidence unearthed through the efforts of forensic accountants is usually the most convincing part of a case brought against white-collar criminals involved in fraud, real estate scams, embezzlement, Ponzi schemes, stock manipulation, and other financial swindles.

Forensic accounting doesn't end there. Investigative numbers crunchers help bring down drug empires, weapons smugglers, loan sharks, illegal gambling operators, money launderers and even terrorists. They also work to untangle financial disputes involving corporations, businesses, estates and divorce cases.

Having a knack for numbers isn't for the faint-hearted anymore. Accountants in the forensic field must have the courage to pursue leads that others may have given up on. They must follow a trail that is long, winding and often frustrating. Accountants who hone their forensic skills must be prepared to see leads they have followed for a while dry up and, undaunted, develop a new trail of clues.

These forensic accounting experts work to solve crimes that perpetrators planned for years with the goal of never being caught – and, if they were apprehended, with an eye toward making any case against them nearly impossible to prove. With that in mind, forensic accountants must keep up with the most advanced investigative techniques, the latest methods used by unscrupulous people to conceal money trails and surreptitious profits, and the newest and boldest scams used to defraud the public and evade law enforcement.

These new age accountants with a zeal for detective work must have a bit of computer geek in them as well. They have to understand how the latest technology works, how they can use it to do their jobs better, and how it can be used against them by those seeking to derail an investigation and make the work of forensic accountants that much tougher.

Once forensic accountants have completed their work, they have to be able to present their findings in a concise and understandable manner, so anyone reviewing the evidence gets a complete understanding of the role money played in the overall case. You may have to work closely with prosecutors over a period of months or even years developing a case, and then present evidence in court.

WHAT YOU CAN DO NOW

ANYBODY WHO WANTS TO GET INTO A career in forensic accounting must first love the accounting process. Taking a high school or college course in introductory accounting is a good place to start. Having a solid grasp of basic accounting principles is essential to setting the stage for a career in money tracking.

Try to get an internship or spend a few hours a week as a volunteer in an accounting office to see if you enjoy working in an atmosphere where you are immersed in numbers all day long, day after day. This will also give you an idea of whether you have the aptitude and personality for this kind of work.

Do some soul searching. Do you enjoy paying attention to details – especially the minute, seemingly insignificant fine points – or do you find this type of work mind-numbing? That's something you should know about yourself before entering this detail-oriented field.

Can you be objective when you are given an assignment? Are you the type of person who can take an unbiased look at a situation and make a judgment based solely on the evidence in the case, without being swayed by outside views, opinions and personalities? That's a requirement in forensic work and you can test yourself easily. When confronted with a problem, do you jump to a conclusion right away? Or do you think like a forensic accountant – taking the time to gather the facts and figuring out how those facts fit together, based on accurate, detailed findings and information?

HISTORY OF THE CAREER

TELEVISION HAS ROMANTICIZED FORENSICS over the past several years. Wall Street scandals have thrust news about secretive money trails, questionable bookkeeping practices and the people who detect them into the headlines on a regular basis. But forensic accountants have been around for decades, making vital contributions to the legal system in countless ways – often unheralded – even helping to provide evidence to convict well-known and dangerous criminals.

The term forensic accountant was first coined by Maurice E. Peloubet, a well-known New York accountant, in the *Journal of Accountancy.* Peloubet wrote an article for the publication in June 1946, titled *Forensic Accounting: Its Place in Today's Economy,* stressing the importance of investigative accounting in society at that time. Even before Peloubet's take on the subject, analytical accounting was being used to track money squirreled away by criminals, only the work was not called forensic accounting.

In the days before his job carried the title forensic accountant, Frank J. Wilson was a renowned investigator with a knack for scrutinizing financial records. For years, law enforcement had been going after crime boss Al Capone for a series of illegal activities in the Chicago area, including murder. All efforts to crush Capone's crime syndicate failed – even investigations conducted by the FBI. In 1929, US Treasury Secretary Andrew Mellon decided to use a recent US Supreme Court decision to put Capone behind bars.

In 1927, the High Court had ruled that gangster Manny Sullivan, who made money from illegal alcohol sales, had to pay income tax on his ill-gotten income. Based on that decision, Mellon ordered Elmer Irey, head of the US Treasury Department's Special Intelligence Unit, to find a way to convict Capone of income tax evasion. To that end, Irey assigned Frank J. Wilson, his best investigator, to the case.

In his book, *The Man Who Got Capone,* author Frank

Spiering quoted Irey as saying of Wilson, "He fears nothing that walks. He will sit quietly looking at books eighteen hours a day, seven days a week. Forever, if he wants to find something in those books." Apparently, Irey was right.

In the summer of 1930, Wilson, along with two of his agents, went through 2 million documents police had confiscated during raids on various operations run by Capone. After months of painstaking work, Wilson found the evidence he needed. He built a meticulous case against the crime kingpin and in June 1931 Capone was indicted by a grand jury on 23 counts of tax evasion. He was convicted on the charges in October 1931 and sentenced to 11 years in prison.

Soon after, the acclaimed Wilson was brought in to work his magic again, this time in the kidnapping case of the Lindbergh baby in 1932. At Wilson's insistence, the serial numbers of the gold certificates used to pay the ransom in the case were recorded before the ransom was paid. Eventually, that led to an arrest and conviction in the case.

Following the success of cases like these, accountants started to be hired to track money trails in both criminal and civil cases. Forensic accounting techniques were used by the US government to track down Swiss bank accounts used by the Nazis during World War II to hide financial assets stolen from victims of the Holocaust. When traced and found, those assets were given back to the victims or their family members.

Gradually, audits began to be used regularly to prove cases of financial wrongdoing, especially when corporate finances were involved. The Internal Revenue Service expanded the way it used investigative accounting to follow money trails. In the 1950s and '60s, all tax cheats became fair game, not just people who committed crimes and failed to pay tax on their financial gains.

Forensics was also gaining credibility as a way to help

untangle finances when it came to divorce and inheritance cases.

By the 1980s, the evidence gathered by forensic accountants was becoming more commonplace in building cases against drug dealers and weapons smugglers. This evidence proved how criminals hid the money they made from these illegal operations.

At the turn of the 21st century, highly publicized corporate financial scandals, like the ones at WorldCom, Tyco, Enron, AIG and Lehman Brothers, were making forensic accountants the superstars of the accounting field. It was left to the expertise of these intrepid investigators to expose unethical accounting practices and the use of bookkeeping loopholes at these corporations to commit fraud.

Now agencies like the Central Intelligence Agency (CIA) are using the talents of forensic accountants in the war on terror. Charged with their most challenging mission to date, forensic financial sleuths are being asked to track the money used by terrorists to fund operations designed to compromise the nation's security.

WHERE THE WORK IS

AS THE NEED FOR FORENSIC ACCOUNTANTS grows, more jobs are being created for them. The most common place for investigative accountants to find work is in large to medium-size accounting firms that do auditing work for corporations. Some accounting firms are specializing exclusively in forensic work. Large law firms, too, have forensic accountants on staff to help in divorce and inheritance cases.

One of the biggest growth areas for employment as a forensic accountant is law enforcement. Though some smaller law enforcement agencies bring in forensic accountants when the need arises, others are starting to employ them on staff. The rise in fraud, plus the need to follow a money trail in certain criminal cases, justifies hiring a full-time financial detective or a team of forensic financial experts.

Just as some large law firms have accounting sleuths on their full-time payroll, district attorney's offices in large cities and counties across the country are also starting to employ forensic accountants full time to help them work with numbers to prove their cases.

Federal government jobs for forensic accountants are growing as well. The FBI, which has worked with accounting detectives for years, is hiring them in greater numbers, as are most other federal law enforcement agencies, including the Bureau of Alcohol, Tobacco and Firearms and the US Secret Service. The Internal Revenue Service (IRS) bolsters its regular accounting staff by employing forensic numbers experts who have the knack and persistence to discover fraud and cover-ups by getting the digits they are scrutinizing to tell them the truth.

Forensic accountants are playing an even bigger role in international intrigue, helping to track the flow of money for numerous illegal enterprises, from the importing of fake designer products from foreign countries for sale in the United States, to illegal drug sales across our nation's borders, and money laundering to cover up funding for terrorist activity. The CIA is using the services of many forensic accountants to crack down on these illegal activities, which threaten the nation's security.

Meanwhile, other federal agencies, such as the Securities and Exchange Commission, the Government Accountability Office, the US Department of the Treasury, and the Federal Trade Commission, call on financial sleuths to conduct investigative work, as do many branches of state government, like departments of banking and insurance.

The banking industry has steadily been increasing its employment of forensic accountants, not just to discover if any irregularities are going on in the financial procedures at a particular bank, but to verify that all banking activities have been conducted correctly. Insurance companies also hire forensic accountants primarily to investigate claims involving financial loss – especially large losses – to make sure each claim is honest and justified. The insurance field is another industry where accounting detectives are handsomely paid to delve into financial records to make sure no illegal activity is going on within the company.

THE WORK YOU WILL DO

IN SIMPLE TERMS, YOUR JOB AS A forensic accountant is to figure out if a fraud or any other financial irregularity took place and, if so, who did it and how. Often easier said than done.

Most frauds and "creative accounting" schemes are complex and can take months, if not years, to fully unearth. Your first task is to establish the scope of the investigation.

Based on information you are given when you are brought in on the case, you have to estimate how long you think the fraud was going on to determine the time period your investigation will cover. This enables you to request the financial records and other documents (emails, memos, cell phone calls) you need to conduct the inquiry. While the scope of the investigation may expand or contract as it goes along, this provides a good starting point.

Develop a time line as you start piecing the evidence together. This will help clarify when events took place and how they played into the overall plot. Make a list of potential suspects as early in the investigation as possible, so you can gather background information on these individuals and be prepared to subpoena their personal financial records, if the need arises.

Try to establish in your mind why the fraud or deceitful action was committed in the first place. This insight will give you a head start on where to look for clues and leads. Who stood to gain from the scheme? Was the act committed for the purpose of stealing funds? Or was it done so the company could "cook the books," to make the business look stronger and more profitable than it really was, or weaker and suffering greater losses?

Your work to uncover the truth will most likely include decoding financial business records designed to cover up misconduct or unlawful behavior and mislead those trying to track it down and bring it to light. The people who devised the scheme – if you know who they are – will probably be uncooperative. So it falls back on the financial detective to break the code in order to prove the case.

Interviewing witnesses is another major part of the investigative process in forensic accounting. That calls for putting together a solid list of people you would be interested in speaking to on a one-to-one basis about the case. These people are not necessarily suspects. Rather, they are individuals who might have been in a position to witness something or have knowledge that could be important to the inquiry. These eyewitness accounts may provide vital leads that paper documents or electronic records cannot.

When looking into corporate frauds or financial irregularities, be sure to learn everything you can about the company you are investigating and the business it's involved in. For instance, try to gain a clear understanding of how the company functions, including knowing where all the corporate offices and facilities are located, how the corporate structure works, the number of employees the company has and their full- or part-time hours, the vendors the corporation purchases from and how they are selected and paid, the banks the company deals with, the terms and length of outstanding loans, what lines of credit the company has, how billings and collections are handled, how payroll is done – all aspects of the business operation may prove useful.

It would also be beneficial to learn all you can about the industry the business you are investigating is part of. For instance, if the target of your probe is in the healthcare field, you should become familiar with the standard operating procedures in the healthcare industry, such as what services are normally provided; the way insurance claims are filed to collect payment; how outside professionals, like therapists, who might be needed in special cases, are hired and the terms of their employment; how outside vendors are selected and contracted for, from cleaning crews to laboratory services; and anything else that is distinctive about that industry's practices and procedures.

When you're reviewing financial records, understanding standard practices in an industry will give you an idea if the company you're looking into veered from the norm or generally stuck with the way business is usually conducted in that field. You are looking for red flags, though just because a company does something a different way doesn't necessarily mean that anything irregular is going on. In fact, most people who commit fraud try to make bookkeeping records look as normal as possible so nothing stands out. That is partly what makes these investigations so difficult.

Armed with deep background information you've collected on the inner workings of the company, its employees and possible reasons for the fraud, you start digging into the firm's financial records. The early focus of the fiscal review will most likely be on the big three financial statements – income, cash flow, and the balance sheet.

These are the records most commonly used by people inside and outside the company to make decisions about the business, and these records are a hot spot for fudging the numbers. Based on these figures, investors and lenders gauge a company's financial fitness, potential partners verify how strong a company really is, labor unions determine profits, government agencies assess tax payments, and suppliers decide whether or not to extend credit to the company.

A great deal of your analysis work will begin with these records and center around them, but these records do not constitute the total picture. Your detective work will expand to numerous other financial documents contained within the company's filing cabinets and computer files, and most likely will spread out to include financial and other records located outside the company in the hands of associates the company does business with.

You may not be able to build your case from information you find in the records of the company at the center of your investigation. The documentation you are looking for might be missing, hidden or destroyed. You may have to develop the proof you need by tracing leads you find in files kept by bankers, vendors and customers who did business with the company under review. These outside sources may have kept records of the transactions that will shed light on a particular irregularity or pattern of wrongdoing. With the data needed to nail down the exact financial irregularities that took place hard to come by solely from company records, documents provided by sources outside the company may at least help you confirm or alter your theories in the case and keep the inquiry alive.

Electronic data must be included in the scope of your investigation, including emails, text messages and any other electronic forms of communication and record keeping. Learn all you can about the latest technology and what it can do. Electronically stored information, often kept in complex computer systems of large companies and simpler systems of smaller businesses, is an excellent source of evidence. You will need to collect all this material and analyze it thoroughly during the course of your investigation. Having a good handle on where critical data is typically hidden within these electronic systems will help speed your review.

Computer backup, recovery or storage systems may also hold some key evidence and must be scrutinized as well. The hard drives of personal computers – some belonging to employees of the company under review, others used by people with outside connections to the company – might have to be searched during the course of the investigation.

As a forensic accountant, you have to be discreet as you take your investigation to sources outside the company. You don't want to cast aspersions on corporate entities, or corporate employees you're not yet sure are doing anything illegal. You may have suspicions, but you have not drawn any firm conclusions yet. You don't have all the proof you need to make a charge.

Some frauds are committed with the help of individuals outside the company, including vendors and subcontractors who also profit from the scheme. You might even find that outside professional consultants hired by the company, such as lawyers or accountants, were involved in the irregularities and intentionally misled some corporate officials, including members of the board of directors.

It is your job to determine how widespread the deception is and to pinpoint all the parties involved. Your investigation cannot leave any unanswered questions, so you must follow all your leads, clearly analyze what you have discovered and draw concrete conclusions.

Once you complete your investigation, you then must present your findings in a report written in simple, easy-to-understand language. This explains what was done, how it was done, who did it, how long it went on, the dollar amounts involved, and how you figured out the scheme. When your explanation is complete, all pieces to the puzzle must fit together.

Your findings have to withstand scrutiny from the legal system if the case winds up in court. You must be able to defend your work, clearly explain how you conducted your investigation, how you came to your conclusions, and what evidence they were based on. That is, you will be asked to prove your case beyond a shadow of a doubt.

Regardless of whether you are probing improprieties in criminal or civil cases, the main focus of forensic accounting efforts is investigative. Forensic accountants working in law enforcement or with a government regulatory agency will be dealing with at least the specter of wrongdoing. These investigations will most likely end with charges being filed or fines being levied.

As a private practitioner, you might find yourself on the other side of these cases – defending your client against government charges and conducting an investigation that will turn up evidence to challenge claims made by the government and exonerate your client. You will review the government's case and search for flaws in the government's investigative process and methods, looking for ways to call into question their figures and findings.

Civil matters for which forensic accountants may be brought in include a variety of heated disputes, tied to years of financial records. The resolution of these disputes may hinge on the unbiased findings of your investigation. Though each side in a d spute may hire a forensic accountant to review the case, more can be accomplished if both sides agree to retain an impartial numbers expert to review the financial records and try to bring the matter to a fair resolution.

Among common civil disputes that benefit from the expertise of a forensic accountant are the dissolution of business partnerships, divorces and estates. In these types of investigations you are usually trying to locate assets that one party might be hiding from the other(s), to avoid having to share them, or determining who brought a particular asset into a partnership or marriage. In the case of divorce, your findings will also be used to help settle disputes over living expenses and child support.

Another aspect of forensic accounting services involves examining financial business records to help a company prevent a fraud from occurring in the first place. This means engaging a fraud examiner to review bookkeeping procedures and determine where a company might be vulnerable to fraud, and then put internal controls in place to avoid having the business victimized. These internal controls need to be updated as the business grows and methods for committing frauds – especially through electronic means – get more sophisticated.

STORIES OF FORENSIC ACCOUNTANTS

I Am Employed By a Government Law Enforcement Agency As a Forensic Accountant

"I like working for the government because the cases we get vary from one to another. There has usually been a fraud committed – that's why we get called in on the case in the first place. That's not always true in the private sector. There, forensic accountants might just be called in to prove that there is no wrongdoing, that everything is in order and has been done properly.

In government law enforcement work, we are involved because someone suspects wrongdoing and has some type of concrete proof that we feel is a starting point for building a case. So right off the bat we are interviewing someone – could be a whistle-blower – who has strong firsthand knowledge of a fraud being committed. Sometimes it's just someone who has suddenly developed a conscience about what has been going on and decides to tell us what has been going on.

If we agree that a crime is being committed, based on what the witness has told us and the evidence presented, we then launch an investigation. These investigations can take quite a while and can involve going through reams of paperwork and years of records – some well-kept, but sometimes a disorganized mess. It is very detail-oriented work.

At first, it is a learning process, just trying to get as much information about the company and/or the person we are investigating. The degree of difficulty in tracking down the fraud usually relates to whether the person committing the crime believes anyone is ever going to notice what is going on and ever going to look into it. If perpetrators feel, 'Oh, nobody's ever going to notice this, no one really cares,' they may be very sloppy in how they cover their trail. A person who thinks they have a real chance of being caught probably takes extra caution in the cover-up, and that fraud is harder to establish and may take even longer to discover by those who are being defrauded.

It all comes down to getting the evidence – getting and developing the leads. At times, we get cooperation, but more often than not we have to get subpoenas to obtain all the records we need.

We usually investigate companies or organizations and people who work for them. We will interview both people within the company and people outside. We talk to employees who may have knowledge of the fraud that is going on, as well as suppliers, customers, creditors, lenders, consultants, and former employees – anyone we feel might have some piece of vital information, whether they know it or not. We never lose sight of the fact that the case might go to trial, and everything we do must stand up in court. So the way we gather evidence and get information can't be compromised or there goes the case."

I Am a Forensic Accountant in Private Practice

"Because of television detective shows I think most people are familiar with the three aspects of crime – means, motive and opportunity – that are needed to convince a jury that a person is guilty of that crime. Well, there is something similar to that when it comes to committing a fraud, and those of us who investigate frauds refer to this as the fraud triangle.

In the case of fraud, the elements involved are pressure, opportunity and rationalization. I like to keep these three elements in mind to help me determine if the person I think might have been involved in the scheme is a viable suspect. It's a good rule of thumb to go by.

Let me explain how this triangle works in the overall investigation. When we talk about pressure, we try to determine if the suspect was under some type of financial stress, like the need to pay gambling debts, that would have led him to develop a scheme to commit a fraud.

Opportunity usually comes from seeing a clear channel to commit this act because the schemer is either in the position to control the books and conceal his actions, or the internal controls in a company are so weak that the plan will simply go undetected. Usually, if you can place the suspect in the role of having control of financial records, it is like being able to put a suspect at the scene of a murder with the murder weapon in his hand.

The rationalization part can be the saddest element of the whole thing, or the most devious. People can justify the fraud in their own mind by believing they are doing it to help a family member or save themselves from financial ruin. They may convince themselves they are actually just borrowing the money and will return it at a later date, so no harm is really being done. Or, they may say to themselves, this company where I work is making so much money, more than they deserve, they can afford to help me out. Then there are those people who feel they were wronged by a company they were working for and committing a fraud is a way of extracting a certain measure of revenge, a way to get even.

These investigations go from looking into a company's financial records to checking the bank accounts of individuals to see if they suddenly came into a financial windfall.

I like to begin every investigation I work feeling that I am completely impartial. I try not to develop feelings or opinions about any of those involved in the investigation.

Sometimes a completely likable person can be guilty, and a totally despicable person can be the victim, the person suffering. I don't want my feelings about a person to control how I investigate a case and the conclusions I draw. You simply can't, that's all there is to it. You must follow the hard evidence and base your findings solely on that. Keeping your personal feelings in check is not always easy to do when you first start out in this field, but you must. It is the only way to do the job justice."

I Am a Forensic Accountant at a Large Accounting Firm

"I handle cases that most people don't realize require a forensic accountant. For instance, if a business is forced to close for any period of time because of a fire or a natural disaster like a flood, a forensic accountant might be called in to help calculate the loss the business suffers. I can figure out the negative financial impact on the business as a result of not being able to operate, which includes lost income as a result of lost sales and production, and the inability to fulfill contracts for goods or services.

There are many other considerations as well, such as damage to business equipment needed for the production of products or running an office, and the cost of replacement; loss of production materials or merchandise; the loss of new and returning consumers; the loss incurred if employees had to be paid while the business was not able to operate; losses if other bills had to paid that relate to employees, like continuing to pay health insurance premiums because the coverage can't be allowed to lapse; losses from ongoing expenses, like rent or business vehicle insurance that has to be paid while no income is being realized; the cost to reopen and bring the business back to where it was before the interruption occurred.

Most businesses carry insurance to cover interruption

of operation, but the claims have to be documented and the insurance companies have forensic accountants on their side to review the claims to make sure they are valid and figured out properly. So, many companies have these claims professionally prepared to make sure they are done correctly and will stand up to scrutiny.

Here's another situation. There's a great deal of litigation that comes out of long drawn-out construction projects where there are heavy cost overruns. Forensic accountants are called in to sort through the litany of invoices and other paperwork involved in these projects to see if these cost overruns are justified. This can involve making sure that billings for fees, overtime, materials and equipment are all proper. Forensic accountants are asked to check out bills for materials to verify that the materials purchased were the ones called for on the job's specifications, that the amount of material ordered was the amount delivered and paid for, that the materials were used on the job in question, if there were materials left over and returned for which a refund was received and properly credited.

We will also check time sheets and make sure everyone paid was actually on the job. If a contractor claims certain losses, we make sure those losses actually occurred. On big construction projects, where there are contractors, subcontractors, architects, engineers and many other people on the job site – and hundreds of millions of dollars involved – there are plenty of opportunities for fraud, and if a legal battle breaks out over costs, it takes a forensic accountant or, at times, several of us to go in and untangle the controversy."

PERSONAL QUALIFICATIONS

A VALUABLE ASSET ANY FORENSIC accountant can have is an inquisitive mind. Each new case is a riddle that needs to be solved. This demands a tireless commitment and the ability to stay focused on the big picture – solving the case.

A financial detective cannot become bored or distracted easily and must be exceedingly detail oriented. At times, the same data has to be reviewed over and over again to spot the irregularity that will begin to shed light on how an illegal money scheme was put together and run. Every lead – some almost imperceptible – has to be followed in this exhaustive search for answers. Someone content with a cursory or casual examination of the evidence, or sloppy inattention to details, will not succeed in this field.

Organization is a vital trait in an investigator sorting through spreadsheets, bank accounts, invoices, billing statements, and related financial records. Keeping copious notes on each document that has been gone through and everything that has been ascertained from reviewing this data is essential to an effective and efficient investigation.

Accounting sleuths often find that they have to review their own work and take a fresh look at the figures, trying to find something they might have overlooked. Having clear, concise notes on how an investigation unfolded helps a forensic accountant conduct an expeditious review of the findings in a case so far, and that may help turn up a new lead.

A healthy degree of skepticism is a good personal trait. This pushes you to question circumstantial evidence before drawing a conclusion. It also means that the forensic accountant demands that all findings be thoroughly supported by documentation – originals, not copies, if possible – before being accepted as facts. More than one form of proof may be required before an investigator is satisfied that a particular point has been proven in a case beyond a reasonable doubt.

An analytical mind is essential when it comes to tracking money. Finding the evidence is only part of the job. Analyzing what this evidence means helps in reconstructing how a crime was committed. The analytical mind can delve into financial records for a certain period, identify patterns and trends in how money matters were conducted, and eventually use those findings to re-create how a fraud was committed.

In this complicated field of financial cover-ups, a love of numbers is not enough. A good forensic accountant must be able to help build a legal case that will withstand tough and bruising questioning in a court of law.

ATTRACTIVE FEATURES

BEING A FORENSIC ACCOUNTANT IS about getting at the truth. An investigation of financial records can prove that a person or corporation did nothing wrong, or it can unearth wrongdoing and potentially send offenders to prison. The facts and figures can back up either conclusion. A financial sleuth can clear someone's name or find allegations of crimes to be true.

Forensic accountants derive much satisfaction in bringing the truth to light, coming to the right conclusion, and playing a pivotal role in seeing justice done. With so much at stake, there is also a great deal of responsibility and prestige that comes with the job. Personal and professional reputations are on the line. The future of a company and its employees often hangs in the balance.

This is a job of consequences and impact. For those who like to be challenged by their work, the field of forensic accounting is the perfect profession. Those hiding an illicit money trail usually put a great deal of thought and planning into the scheme they devise, and unraveling it can be difficult. It usually takes every bit of know-how an accountant has to develop a case that is not only legally sound, but one that a jury will be able to understand.

The work is never routine. Though the practices used to conceal financial fraud may be similar from one case to the next, they are rarely identical, which will make your work always interesting and challenging. Determining the exact means by which someone hid ill-gotten monetary gains can lead you on a wild numerical adventure.

The work of accountants is highly valued, their opinion is sought, they are an integral part of an investigative team, and they may get an opportunity to break a case wide open by locating a small shred of   evidence that may otherwise go unnoticed. When it comes to corporate fraud and other money-based crimes, it is often the forensic accountant who answers the question, "How'd they do it?"

Success in investigative accounting can also lead to other opportunities for those with a flair for teaching and writing. There is a need for those who have put together a long and distinguished career in the forensic accounting field to teach their skills to others looking to go into this rapidly growing field. Writing about your cases, trends in the field, methods developed to unearth financial schemes, techniques used to foil accounting fraud, and a variety of other related topics are all solid subjects for accounting journal articles and books.

UNATTRACTIVE FEATURES

FRUSTRATION! IT COMES WITH ANY investigative work. You will invest weeks, even years of hard work following a lead that just doesn't pan out. You will have times when several leads all end up going nowhere. That means starting all over again. Finding new leads, forging a new path. If you tire easily of trying to find new ways of looking at the same case, forensic accounting will be difficult for you.

Usually, people using numbers to commit a crime conceal their actions well. They may have some accounting expertise themselves, and they plan ahead by thinking of ways to throw a forensic accountant off their trail if someone discovers the fraud and decides to call in the experts to figure it out. A clever schemer may even drop some red herrings into the plot just to make it that much more difficult for investigators to crack the case.

It can take a long time until you see any progress in a case and a longer time until you can declare success with any certainty. Intrepid money trackers put in long hours on the job during an ongoing investigation. Leads are not followed simply on a nine-to-five basis. Investigators burn the midnight oil, work on weekends and are even tied to their desks during holidays, all in an effort to crack a difficult case.

When a fraud has been perpetrated against a large number of unsuspecting people, when a corporation's future is teetering on the brink of ruin because of ongoing financial shenanigans, there can be a great deal of pressure on a forensic accountant to get to the bottom of what's going on in a short amount of time. Not everyone is comfortable working under this kind of pressure. When people are being defrauded, they want answers now and if that's not the kind of working environment you can handle, it can become overwhelming.

In many fraud cases, an extensive investigation is conducted, evidence is gathered and the case that is put together is so strong that it is practically impossible for those being accused to mount a plausible defense. But there are those instances where a case will wind up in court and the forensic accountant who worked on the case will be called to testify as an expert witness. Testifying in court is difficult and stressful. Some people simply do not handle the courtroom experience well. It can take time to prepare to present your findings and also prepare to defend your conclusions under withering cross-examination.

EDUCATION AND TRAINING

WITH US NEWS & WORLD REPORT CALLING it one of the eight careers you can count on, forensic accounting is getting a great deal of attention from job seekers. When everybody starts migrating to a particular field, it's advisable to get the type of education and training that will make you stand out among other eager candidates.

First, you will need to become an accountant. There are many colleges that offer bachelor's degrees in accounting. Learning everything you can about accounting will prepare you to further hone your skills in the forensic specialty.

Community colleges offer two-year associate degrees in accounting, and that is a good place to start your education. Most federal agencies, however, require a four-year college degree in accounting to gain employment as a forensic accountant, and many companies in the private sector do as well.

Being a knowledgeable general accountant is not enough to build a reputation in forensic work. Students should consider augmenting their accounting skills with courses in business basics. Forensic accountants will find it easier to unearth clues to business fraud with a clear understanding of how commerce operates. So an accounting degree program with a business minor would serve you well. Taking courses in business law and investigative techniques is also worthwhile. This kind of education can continue even after you graduate from college with an accounting degree.

A few colleges, like Carlow University, a private Catholic University in Pittsburgh, offer a bachelor's degree in forensic accounting. The Carlow program combines an accounting minor with courses such as fraud investigation techniques, criminology, ethics, fraud examination and principles of finance.

Georgia Southern University in Statesboro, Georgia has extensive courses in fraud and forensic accounting on both the undergraduate and graduate levels.

While graduate degrees in forensic accounting are scarce at this point, the State University of New York (SUNY) at Albany does offer a one-year master's degree program in forensic accounting. St. Thomas University in St. Paul, Minnesota awards a master's of accounting degree with a specialization in forensic accounting. The University of Charleston in West Virginia has an executive master of forensic accounting program at its Graduate School of Business. An advanced certificate in forensic accounting is available at the John Jay College of Criminal Justice in New York City.

Many business colleges, like Strayer University and DeVry University, have in their curriculums extensive courses in both general and forensic accounting – both at campus locations and online. The online option gives people who have to work full time an opportunity to study in their spare time.

Regardless of where you get your accounting degree, you will have to take the test to become a licensed certified public accountant (CPA) in your state if you want to pursue a career in forensic accounting. Though not a requirement for some career paths in accounting, a CPA license is prized in the forensics field. With a CPA license, it's easier for you to get a job interview, even on the entry level. This credential indicates an in-depth knowledge of accounting and a high standard of professionalism.

Most states offer courses to help prepare for the CPA exam. In the years following the exam, you will also have to meet continuing education requirements, some of which may be in the forensic accounting specialty. Many of the continuing education courses are presented by professional organizations like the National Association of Forensic Accountants, the Association of Certified Fraud Examiners and the American Board of Forensic Accounting.

For instance, the Association of Certified Fraud Examiners (ACFE) hosts conferences and seminars on the latest techniques in fraud prevention and investigation. In addition, the association has online continuing education training as well as on-site courses at certain large accounting firms or agencies involved in the forensic accounting field.

The ACFE is one of the few professional organizations in the field that offers its members a certification and recertification process. To become a certified fraud examiner (CFE), you have to pass a CFE test and have all the documentation attesting to your educational and professional qualifications. The test is exhaustive, and the association offers an instructor-led course as well as a manual to help candidates prepare for the exam. Other associations in the field have certifications as well.

Some four-year colleges with top general accounting programs:

New York University
New York City

University of Pennsylvania Philadelphia

Indiana University
Bloomington, Indiana

University of Southern California Los Angeles

University of Michigan
Ann Arbor

University of Washington, Seattle

Brigham Young University
Provo, Utah

University of Notre Dame
South Bend, Indiana

EARNINGS

FORENSIC ACCOUNTING IS HAVING A surge. It is one of the few fields today where demand outpaces supply in the workforce, so the earnings potential is high in this burgeoning profession. Entry-level jobs start between $40,000 and $60,000 a year. After a few years in the field, with the proper experience, a forensic accountant can easily start earning six figures and move up from there.

Jobs in the private sector pay more than government jobs, but the number of fraud-related crimes perpetrated on Wall Street and in major corporations has the government doing more to guard against and investigate these breaches in trust. That means that forensic accountants who work for the government are getting jobs at higher pay levels.

In addition, the experience gained by working for the government makes fraud investigators more valuable when they decide to leave public service and look for work in the private sector. There they can command higher salaries than those who never worked for the government.

Other factors drive up salaries in this field as well. Becoming a Certified Fraud Examiner, for instance, may entitle you to a salary roughly 20 percent higher. Other continuing education credits, memberships in professional organizations and accreditations can lead to raises in earnings. Recognition as a good expert witness can also yield financial rewards. It is difficult to find knowledgeable and gifted forensic accountants who are also comfortable testifying in court. Those who have this talent are paid handsomely.

OPPORTUNITIES

THE GREED OF MODERN DAY CRIMINALS has created unlimited opportunities for forensic accountants and undoubtedly will continue to help the profession grow. Over the last decade, there has been no greater outcry from elected officials, investors and the public at large than the need to stop the seemingly free flow of fraud and scams plaguing the nation. Using forensic accountants to crack down on these offenders has been one of the ways that government and law enforcement have tried to stem the tide of this alarming epidemic.

A significant piece of legislation addressing this crisis, the Sarbanes-Oxley Act, became law in 2002. Praised for promoting a new ethic of corporate responsibility, this law made sweeping changes in independent audits, accounting services and financial reporting for public companies. The law was designed to provide steep penalties for corporate and accounting fraud and corruption. The law, however, is only as effective as those who track down the violators and bring them to justice.

For forensic accountants, this means even more work – both in big cities and small towns. Most large to medium-size accounting firms have created special fraud investigation divisions. Boutique accounting firms are beginning to spring up to handle forensic accounting issues exclusively. These specialty investigative bookkeeping firms are the fastest-growing segment of the accounting industry today for people who want to start their own businesses.

Based on the success that forensic accounting has achieved in ferreting out corporate fraud, the same techniques are now being used in a variety of fiscal matters – both commercial and private – to make sure financial records are complete, correct and honest. For instance, if two companies are merging, even if they are both privately held, an independent forensic accountant is often brought in these days to make sure the books kept by both companies are in order.

It is generally recognized that if you want to get to the bottom of financial irregularities – or make sure there aren't any – you call in a forensic accountant. That has made forensic accounting what *SmartMoney* magazine called one of the 10 hottest jobs in the country.

Forensic accountants are in demand all over the country and beyond. The United States is not the only country where forensic accountants are employed. Many nations, including Canada, England, Australia and Ireland, have these professionals working in both the private and public sector.

International business ventures also rely heavily on the input and findings of the forensic specialists of the accounting profession. Because there is such a high demand, those entering the field over the next decade will have abundant opportunities to get valuable, on-the-job experience investigating cases of all kinds. Easier cases will allow young accounting investigators to develop their skills. Those who stand out will be able to move up as the need for management and investigative leaders grows as the field expands.

GETTING STARTED

WHEN YOU ARE STARTING OUT IN THIS CAREER, IT IS NOT about how much you can make – it is about how much you can learn. Experience today will help you earn a great deal more in the future. Internships are always a good place to start, especially if you can land a couple while you are still in school. There is no substitute for real-life, on-the-job experience, and these internships give you solid job experience to list on your résumé. Try to get an internship that not only relates to accounting but includes job-related experience in fraud investigation as well. Seeing experienced investigators conduct investigative fieldwork firsthand will be an eye-opener.

When you enter the job market, keep in mind that one of the best places to gain experience in the growing field of forensic accounting is in a government job. With so many branches of government committed to cracking down on fraud, there are many jobs available. Though these jobs don't pay as much as jobs in private enterprise, they do offer you an opportunity to work on a wide variety of cases and give you a perspective you probably won't get at a private accounting firm.

Government investigations usually involve much more than just taking a long, hard look at the numbers. They also call for you to learn the methodology of developing a case. Building a strong case is an important aspect of forensic accounting. If you put together a sloppy case, you usually end up losing in court.

The government doesn't like to look foolish and doesn't like to lose, so government agencies will usually take their time and take great pains to put together a convincing case. Being part of that process will help you learn the ins and outs of making an effective courtroom presentation, as well as the proper way to collect and inventory evidence.

Government officials usually conduct a number of interviews when performing investigations. The art of the effective interview in fraud cases is something you can only learn by witnessing an interview in progress or being involved in the process itself. No classroom experience can prepare you for the unexpected twists and turns that happen during actual interviews of witnesses in a case.

The information acquired from these interviews, often given inadvertently, can shed a different light on a case than that gained just by examining documents. Learning how to work with witnesses is an extremely valuable skill. The array of cases the government has will give you a good cross section of witnesses to work with and interview.

Working with government agencies like the IRS, the FBI, and the Securities and Exchange Commission gives you an opportunity to learn about government regulations and how they are enforced and even developed. These insights are tremendously valuable if you decide to take your talents to the private sector and work cases where you might have to defend a client against those same regulations, or perhaps challenge the law itself. Government experience is also considered a strong credential on a résumé when you are seeking employment in the private sector.

ASSOCIATIONS

- **Association of Certified Fraud Examiners (ACFE)**
www.acfe.com

- **National Association of Forensic Accountants (NAFA)**
www.nafanet.com

- **International Forensic Accounting Association (IFAA)**
www.forensicaccountingassociation.com

- **American Board of Forensic Accounting/American College of Forensic Examiners**
www.abfa.us

- **Forensic CPA Society (FCPA)**
www.fcpas.org

- **American Institute of Certified Public Accountants (AICPA)** www.aicpa.org

- **National Association of Certified Valuators and Analysts (NACVA)**
www.nacva.com

- **American Accounting Association**
www.aaahq.org

PERIODICALS

- **Journal of Forensic Accounting**

- **The Forensic Examiner**

- **Practical Accounting Magazine**

- **Global Forensics**

- **Accountants World Daily Newsletter**

- **Accounting Today**

- **Journal of Accountancy**

- **SmartMoney**

- **The CPA Journal**

- **Journal of Accounting Research**

WEBSITES

- http://www.cpajournal.com

- http://www.icaew.com/en/library**/subject-gateways/law/forensic-accounting**

- http://www.academy-experts.org/

- **Most states have a society of certified public accountants, with a useful website that contains information and breaking news about the accounting and forensic accounting industries in that state, as well as job openings. As examples, see the New York State Society of Certified Public Accountants (www.nysscpa.org) and the Vermont Society of Certified Public Accountants (www.vtcpa.org)**

www.ingramcontent.com/pod-product-compliance
Lightning Source LLC
Chambersburg PA
CBHW07075218052
45168CB00004B/1594